Wildlife Watchers

Ruby Tuesday Readers

Blackbird

By Ruth Owen

Educational Consultant:
Dee Reid

Tips for Reading with Your Child

- Set aside at least 10 to 15 minutes each day for reading.
- Find a quiet place to sit with no distractions. Turn off the TV, music and screens.
- Encourage your child to hold the book and turn the pages.
- Before reading begins, look at the pictures together and talk about what you see.
- If the reader gets stuck on a word, try reading to the end of the sentence. Often by reading the word in context, he or she will be able to figure out the unknown word. Looking at the pictures can help, too.
- Words shown in **bold** are explained in the glossary on pages 22–23.

Above all enjoy the time together and make reading fun!

Book Band Orange

For more information about blackbirds go to: www.rubytuesdaybooks.com/wildlifewatchers

What do you know about blackbirds?

Why does a blackbird sing?

- To make a nice sound.
- To protect its home.
- To wake people up.

What does a blackbird build her nest from?

- Grass, twigs and mud
- Bricks and wood
- Spiderwebs

What do blackbird chicks eat?

- Fish and chips
- Mice and lizards
- Worms and insects

What do blackbirds eat in winter?

- Porridge
- Berries and fruit
- Soup

Now read this book and find the answers.

It's a warm evening in summer.

A blackbird is singing in a garden.

He sings to tell other male blackbirds to keep away.

The blackbird sees another male on the grass.

He chases him away.

The garden is the blackbird's **territory** and he will chase away any other males.

The blackbird lives with a female blackbird.

She is his **mate**.

The female is building a **nest**.

She picks up grass and small twigs in her beak.

She picks up mud to stick the grass and twigs together.

The female blackbird builds her nest in two weeks.

Then she lays four little blue eggs in the nest.

The blackbird sits on her eggs to keep them warm.

After 14 days there is a tap, tap, tap!

What can it be?

A blackbird chick hatches from its egg.

It has fluffy, grey feathers called **down**.

Soon, three more chicks hatch from their eggs.

The baby birds can't see because their eyes have not opened yet.

The chicks are very, very hungry!

The parent blackbirds must find lots of worms and **insects** for their chicks to eat.

The father bird looks for worms in the grass.

He picks up lots of fat worms in his beak.

He flies to the nest and feeds the worms to the chicks.

Every day the mother and father birds bring food to the chicks.

Soon, the chicks' eyes open and their feathers start to grow.

When they are two weeks old, the chicks jump out of the nest.

The baby birds can't fly yet.

They hop around the garden.

The baby blackbirds are in danger!

A cat is hunting for birds in the garden.

The chicks can't fly away from the cat.

The brave father blackbird attacks the cat!

Chink Chink Chink

He gives his angry call.

Then he flies at the cat again and again.

The cat is scared and it runs away.

The chicks grow bigger, but they still beg their father for food.

Where is the mother blackbird?

She has laid more eggs and she is keeping them warm!

The chicks like to eat worms and insects, but they will eat fruit, too.

When they are five weeks old, they can fly and take care of themselves.

All summer the blackbirds take care of their chicks.

When winter comes, the chicks fly away and the parent blackbirds are all alone in the garden.

Now there are no worms or insects to eat, so they eat fruit and **berries**.

Soon it will be spring and time for more blackbird chicks!

Glossary

berry
A small fruit that grows on a tree or other plant.

down
Soft, thin feathers on the body of a baby bird.

insect
A small animal with six legs and a body in three parts.

mate
An animal's partner with which it has babies.

nest
A home where animals live or take care of their babies.

territory
The place where an animal lives, finds its food and finds a mate.

Blackbird Quiz

1. How many eggs did the female blackbird lay?

2. How would you describe a baby blackbird that has just hatched?

3. How did the father blackbird protect his babies from a cat?

4. What is happening in the picture on page 20?

5. How old are the chicks when they are ready to take care of themselves?